Nursery Rhymes

by
Deepika Sardana
M.A. (Eng.)

D. S. Publishers (India)

E-1,16 Darya Ganj
New Delhi - 110 002
India
+91 (11) 6525 3158, 3290 1695
ds_bookmaster@yahoo.co.in

RING-A-RING O' ROSES

Ring-a-ring o' roses,
A pocket full of posies,
A-tishoo! A-tishoo!
We all fall down.

TEDDY BEAR, TEDDY BEAR

Teddy bear, Teddy bear,
Turn around;
Teddy bear, Teddy bear,
Touch the ground.
Teddy bear, Teddy bear,
Polish your shoes;
Teddy bear, Teddy bear,
Off to school.

JOHNNY, JOHNNY

Johnny, Johnny,
Yes, papa.
Eating sugar?
No, papa.
Telling lies?
No, papa.
Open your mouth.
Ha! Ha! Ha!

TIK - TIK - TIK

Tik - tik - tik,
The clock goes tik - tik,
Oh! I should hurry up,
To go to school quick.

TWINKLE, TWINKLE

Twinkle, twinkle, little star,
How I wonder what you are!
Up above the world so high,
Like a diamond in the sky!

EARLY TO BED

Early to bed
And early to rise,
Makes a child healthy,
Wealthy and wise.

TOMY WENT TO A FAIR

Tomy went to a fair,
And sat on a mare,
The mare ran very fast,
Tomy fell down at last.

A B C

A B C
Tumble down D.
The cat's in the cupboard,
And cannot see me.

PUSSY CAT, PUSSY CAT

Pussy cat, pussy cat,
Where have you been?
I've been to London,
To visit the Queen.

Pussy cat, pussy cat,
What did you there?
I frightened a little mouse,
'Neath the Queen's chair.

CHUBBY CHEEKS

Chubby cheeks, dimpled chin,
Rosy lips, teeth within,
Curly hair, very fair,
Eyes are blue, lovely too,
Teacher's pet, is that you?
Yes, Yes, Yes!

THE MOON

I see the moon,
The moon sees me.
God bless the moon,
And God bless me.

LITTLE JACK HORNER

Little Jack Horner sat in a corner,
Eating a Christmas pie;
He put in his thumb,
And pulled out a plum,
And said, “What a good boy am I!”

ONE, TWO, THREE, FOUR

One, two, three, four,
Mary at the cottage door;
Five, six, seven, eight,
Eating cherries off a plate.

MY TEACHER MARY

My teacher Mary,
Is very sweet,
She takes us to picnic,
And gives chocolates to eat.

JACK AND JILL

Jack and Jill went up the hill,
To fetch a pail of water;
Jack fell down, and broke his crown,
And Jill came tumbling after.

MY CUTE GRANNY

My cute granny,
Sweet-sweet granny,
She tells me lovely stories,
Of prince, princess, and fairies.

TRING - TRING - TRING

Tring - tring - tring,
The telephone rings,
Its from my granny,
I would go, if I had wings.

HUMPTY DUMPTY

Humpty Dumpty sat on a wall,
Humpty Dumpty had a great fall;
All the King's horses and all the King's men,
Couldn't put Humpty Dumpty together again.

THE SKY ON THE TOP

The sky on the top,
Down is ground,
Who made this lovely world,
And the earth so round.

RAINBOW, RAINBOW

Rainbow, Rainbow
Here comes rainbow,
It has got seven rows,
Of colours called VIBGYOR.